Freedom from Fear

A Guided Introduction to Shadow Work

Dedication

I dedicate this book to my incredibly supportive beloved grandparents.

To whom, before the world told me I was dyslexic, purchased me a grey Brothers typewriter. I said I wanted to be a writer and write short stories. I was in alignment with my soul's purpose then, and I'm now. I Thank you for doing whatever it took for me to follow my dreams at all times.

CONTENTS

INTRODUCTION

I'm not going to make any promise to you. The facts are I don't know if this book will change your life or even shift your mindset. What I know is it was written with the height intentions to help you reconnect with your highest form of light and love within. It depends on applying what you are learning and embracing a new version of yourself while moving forward with the old in the highest form of light and love. I Trust you will approach this process with acceptance and allowance. I need you to know we are co-creating a fearless life for you. Friends, this book is to be used as a loose blueprint for you to forge your shadow work path. To be completely honest, my friends, none of our experiences will mirror each other. Frankly, it's not met, so we are uniquely created to be the best version of ourselves. When we find peace within ourselves, we see that our uniqueness is the beauty of life's experience. We all have been individually blessed to be who we are, which is our gift to each other. That's why this work is so important; too many of us have been trying not to stand out, making us stagnant, and delivering our gifts to the world is extremely difficult with no momentum. When you show up in a world that is released from fear and full of love, we can move forward more cohesively towards peace, understanding, joy, and abundance. Most importantly, we can have grace and acceptance of one another now!

Next steps, let's learn to create a life free of fear consciously. I intend to HELP every reader find and FALL in love with their authentic voice with the use of shadow work. Within the core of this book are questions that will leave you feeling exposed. I am a strong believer in therapy. I think it's very important to be selective in finding a therapist to help you maintain your mental strength and clarity. It's a lifetime of necessary work . We fuel our bodies with the proper foods. We spend time maintaining our physical goals. Having a therapist you can meet with, even if it's just once a month, Makes a world of difference in one's life and lifestyle. Therapy has helped equip me to write this book being completely transparent.

Take what you need now and leave the rest for later.

We don't get all mature; just because we take advantage of frequent turns around the sun. This shadow work process can be quite triggering. Please, friends, seek a professional if you feel overwhelmed or triggered. If you allow yourself to show up for this work truly, it can and will get dark at times; forge through my friend's freedom is on the other side!

Being completely transparent, my journey was dark, and it was quiet. I felt a deep sense of isolation and understanding. I remember getting on the other side and saying I wish I was better prepared and had more tools. My perfectionist energy shone through, trying to control a spiritual awakening girl bye! Being the healer I am, I have to give you some tools. I have equipped you with some tools you can run to any moment for security stability, a reset, or a renewal of energy. Energy has to be intentionally transmuted. Please use the tools below as needed to balance the dark and light within.

TIME FOR PEACE AND PROTECTION EXPLAINED:

BODY (3)

Breath Work

When you see "breath work" in the book, take a pause. At this time, take slow, very intentional three-count breaths. Long deep, and internal inhales and exhales. Allow the emotions and energy in motion to be transmuted and used to serve you!

Soul (2)

Crystals

Let's be honest; we release fears when we feel more protected. At the end of every chapter, I list two protective crystal recommendations and their healing properties.

Mind (1)

Affirmation

I feel Affirmations are great for shifting the mind and empowering oneself. While simultaneously transmuting energy at the moment, helping to improve emotions. I will include an empowering affirmation at the end of every chapter.

TIME FOR PEACE AND PROTECTION:

Breath work: (3)

- Breathe In, count to three slowly, and fill your lungs!

- Now, hold your breath for three seconds

- Release, slowly exhale for three seconds

- Now, smile or laugh no matter your current emotions!

Crystal: (2)

Hematite

A protective stone that can absorb negative energy. It helps to stay grounded in times of worry and stress by balancing the mind, body, and spirit.

Pink Tourmaline

Love emotional healing. Helps repair holes in the auric field from emotional wounds.

Affirmations:(1)

I have the tools I need to make the most of this new beginning.

THE BEAUTY OF CO-CREATION

Let's co-create, setting our intentions on empowering ourselves. The goal is to align with the highest versions of one's highest self. Friend, I believe the sooner we deal, the soon we heal. I will not lie; your commitment is required. This process will be extremely dark and challenging at times. However, In the midst of my shadow work journey, I found my unapologetic loving voice. My goal is to guide you down a new path to knowing and recognizing your voice. It's important to know your voice. When we identify our voice, we act with more intention. Set proper boundaries with ourselves and others. In turn, significantly impact the world around us from a healed perspective. Accountability through the eyes of alignment while simultaneously acknowledging your purpose and path is a life of freedom. Our goal is to let the overwhelming feeling of fear go. Leaving dis-ease, lack, and resistance in the past. Walking a path seeking ease and peace. With the help of all the right questions and a hunger for a life without fear, we will grow and glow by the end of our co-created shadow work path!

My Goal is to equip you with the questions for you to begin the shadow work process. I intend to encourage, energize, and empower every reader. After my first deep dive into my shadow work journey, I fully aligned with my purpose. This is my purpose; I am honored to be your partner in crime for you to start your deep dive into your shadow work path. Now it's not about me; it's about you! I will encourage you to work slowly. Trust the process, and take part in the suggested breath work embedded in every chapter. The breath work will bring you back into your body and the now. The crystals hold power to leave you energized if you decide to add them to your collection or start a new collection. I believe our words matter and help to mold our thinking patterns, beliefs, and behaviors. Empowering affirmation will also be included at the end of every chapter to enhance our mindset. I trust you will leave this reading experience feeling equipped to begin your shadow work journey. I have faith that this is all Divine timing! You will start the work, and when you do the job, you will feel empowered.

Friends, let's back up; you are probably asking yourself, Who Is T.C, and why Is she qualified to help guide me through my beginning stages of shadow work? Spreading love and light is a part of my purpose. I have such freedom now that I can hardly put it into words. It feels like fear can not control my life nor paralyze me. It feels like being present is the key to keeping my happiness. It feels like a life led with a spirit of gratitude and abundance is my only option, the only life I'm choosing daily. My shadow work journey had to happen. It was divine timing, and now, you have picked up this book, and it is your divine timing. I'm happy to be here and able to support you on your path. Shadow work helped me understand that all the bad things that happen to me are for my highest good and that everything good that happens to me is also for my heights good. I Embrace this understanding and find peace, joy, and love within. I leave fear behind in a book I no longer use for my entertainment. It exists; however, I'm no longer a vibrational match for the stories within it. I choose not to open and engage. My past and ongoing detection of the shadow work process makes me equipped and qualified. Congratulations on showing up for yourself; now, let's begin!

TIME FOR PEACE AND PROTECTION:

Breath work: (3)

- Breathe In, counting to three slowly, and fill your lungs!
- Now, hold your breath for three seconds
- Release, slowly exhale for three seconds
- Now, smile or laugh no matter your current emotions!

Crystal :(2)

Black Obsidian

Absorbs negativity and establishes a strong sense of self. Reveals deeper truths.

Jade

Sacred healing stone with clearing and blessing energies. Reducing tension and encouraging balance and self-conference. Jade keeps you connected to your inner peace and helps clarify and clear negative emotions.

Affirmation:(1)

I let go of the past and have faith in the future.

CHAPTER 2

SHADOW WORK, NO RAIN, NO ROSES

Why did you purchase this book? How do you intend to feel after reading his book? Have you set your intentions already to do the work? Are you prepared to honestly answer the difficult questions? I had to identify and uncover my true story. I had to permit myself to see what I had spent years avoiding and suppressing . What I have decided to embrace during my shadow work path is that I have to make my inner and outer child happy to find and walk in my purpose. I had to uncover and release all the stories I have lived the past 35 years trying to prove. I had to let go of the limiting beliefs. I had to believe in myself again. I had to believe in a new narrative, I had set for myself. I have spent decades embodying other peoples limiting beliefs about my life. I'm free from that weight. I am free from the fears people projected on my life. I choose my thoughts and feelings by feeling them and communicating my true desires. I honor my No's! I don't answer the phone when I don't feel like talking. I create boundaries and honor them at all times. I'm just unwilling to expose myself to dis-ease to make others comfortable. Most importantly, I have found freedom from fear by letting go of the past and showing up to every moment with nothing but my authentic self, voice, and feelings. Let me tell you; I AM living! I take shadow work extremely seriously. I take my mindset extremely seriously, and you should to my friend!

I spend time looking up the definition of words to ensure the words I'm using are based on their true definition and not my worldly definition. Our past experiences can make us delusional. You must be present, my friends and I suggest you slow down and trust. You have to connect with how we feel. This work is crucial to releasing fear and finding happiness.

Allow me to give you an example of this process. This is how I defined this word because of the world and all of my past experiences; this is what the true definition. What does this make me feel? Why does it make me feel this way? Is there an experience from my past that has influenced my current feelings? What are the facts about this? How do I desire to feel?

Shadow work makes us more aware of what our true desires are and what is worth our energy. We will take time to step back into our childhood memories and release any existing connections and attachments that no longer serve us and are not in alignment with the person we are diligently working to become. I ask that you keep an open mind and heart. Mainly heart, how do I feel? Opposed to mind, what do I think? Please prepare yourself for the surrender; letting go is a major part of shadow work.

Shadow work is taking the time to explore our dark side and fighting fear with facts! It takes an enormous amount of courage to embark on this inner journey. Shadow work is peeling back the layers of memories and emotions within. Exploring past experiences, especially in our adolescence. Identifying how different events and small situations have impacted and influenced our lives today. The impact on our thoughts, patterns, habits, emotions, behaviors, traits, and communication styles. Now, friends, this work is impactful because this is all done by working with the unconscious and subconscious minds. Much of our fear is rooted in our insecurities, attachment patterns, and coping and avoidance patterns. Shadow work helps us identify and release identity and restore identity and renew as required. I am grateful for this process. I have abundant peace, joy, self-awareness, understanding, and acceptance. The best part, my friend, is fear no longer leaves me paralyzed. Allow room to separate from your ego and get in more alignment with LOVE. This process is lifelong, and in different seasons it will get dark and difficult, and that's okay. Friend, come back to the beginning, take a deep breath, and start where you are. Do this work scared!

TIME FOR PEACE AND PROTECTION:

Breath work: (3)

- Breathe In, counting to three slowly, and fill your lungs!
- Now, hold your breath for three seconds
- Release, slowly exhale for three seconds
- Now, smile or laugh no matter your current emotions!

Crystal :(2)

Black Aegirine

protection and strength of convictions.

Lepidolite

Calms the mind and removes negativity. Restores self-value, self-respect, and self-reliance

Affirmation:(1)

I Am true to myself at all times.

CHAPTER 3

BRING NOTHING, THE PROBLEM WITH NOSTALGIA

It is important to realize when your subconscious is at the root of your daily actions and choices. What I realized in my own shadow work experience is, on a subconscious level, I lived in fear and was always looking to prevent and protect myself instead of just living in the moment and trusting. Reminder fear is false evidence appearing real. We can never guarantee what's gonna happen in the future. Mainly because the future isn't guaranteed. To live in fear in regard to the unknown is dangerous. It's time to surrender; it's time to take risks and experience freedom. The Fear of reliving how something made me feel in the past left me feeling paralyzed, trapped in my own thoughts! Our thoughts form our beliefs and collectively frame our day-to-day life. If we live with fear and worry about reliving past emotions such as hurt, fear, and or past trauma, our choice, and decisions reflect that daily. On an energetic level, we are putting ourselves back in that past place unnecessarily. The fear kicked in because I didn't process my true feelings. I didn't deal I didn't heal. I chose to avoid and suppress how I felt. Once I process my feelings, I identify the facts and give myself permission to let go, surrender, and release fear; the false evidence no longer appears real. I AM worthy of letting go and embracing a fresh start. You are worthy! Are you ready is the question. We can release the bondage and blockages we keep deep in our subconscious; we can release fear now. This work is extremely triggering; please work alongside a therapist when you feel overwhelmed and or throughout the entire process. I'm not a licensed professional; I'm just telling my story in hopes of equipping, encouraging, and empowering my readers to begin the difficult self-efficacy work.

Let me leave you with this example from my personal experience with this difficult process. When I was younger, my grandparents would pick me up from school late. Like mad late! My teachers had to stay behind and wait for me to get picked up. Before they could start their weekend, after being released from their professional duties as a teacher. Before enjoying their well-deserved personal time off. On a subconscious level, that experience made me feel like an inconvenience. I would always feel like people were waiting for me to leave. I always felt I was on the verge of overstaying my welcome. I approached a lot of situations with that energy. The energy was rooted in the false narrative that I was a major inconvenience to the people around me. I Embodied this energy in all of my relationships and interactions. This mindset made me not appreciate and feel grateful for the people around me. Not allow space for my own self expression and or room for connection. Due to the fact that I was focusing more on trying to find the perfect time to leave. I was never fully present in every moment with the people around me. For a deeper understanding when I say people I mean family friends and complete strangers. Just drowning in angst and internal worry! Analyzing my every move, never fully listening. I knew I needed a shift if I was ever going to experience any true happiness. I was buried alive in a false negative limiting belief. I asked myself, How do I stop this behavior how do I move forward? I knew I needed to let go of these patterns ,this way of thinking before my thoughts manifested into internal physical illness. That is when my journey started; I decided to surrender then in that moment. This is just one example of the false narratives I lived with before starting my Shadow work journey. How do I feel today in these same environments? Now my friend, I know I'm worthy of people's time and energy! Now I permit myself to take up space! On more challenging days, I stop my negative narrative mid thought . I focus on what the facts are in all situations. Then I pause and list them off. I feel better after I take a few deep breaths and say a few affirmations that help to encourage me to make a mental shift with discernment and patience and, most importantly, love. I feel freedom, I feel peace,

I feel safe, and I trust the process of life. Most importantly, I let go of fear.

I had to comment on doing the work. I had to get vulnerable and dig deep into my childhood. The shadow work process will take you to some old yet raw emotions (energy in motion). It's important to transmute this energy. That's where the healing comes into place. That's when you feel the freedom! Are you ready to comment to yourself, my friend?

I asked you to bring nothing with you, my friend. Everything you need is inside of you. This book focuses on how we feel, not what we think! We are no longer making people's false images, negative narratives, the scripts to live our lives by. It's time to take over the stage. There is only room for one star in this show, and that is you! The only person who has permission to write a script about your life is you! It's time to take control of your life, my friend. It's time to renew, restore, and or release any relationships that do not bring you joy and peace, including the most important relationship, the one with self. It's time to take the stage, please bring your main character energy from here on out in life!

TIME FOR PEACE AND PROTECTION:

Breath work: (3)

- Breathe In, count to three slowly, and fill your lungs!
- Now, hold your breath for three seconds
- Release, slowly exhale for three seconds
- Now, smile or laugh no matter your current emotions!

Crystal :(2)

Black Onyx

A powerful protective crystal absorbs, blocks, and cleanses negative energy. Provides emotional healing and infuses you with feelings of joy, hope, and positivity.

Malachite

Enhance inner insight, spiritual growth, and transformation. Absorbing negative pollutants from both the atmosphere and the body.

Affirmation:(1)

I let go of the past and have faith in the future.

CHAPTER 4

THE BEAST IN THE SHADOWS

Time to peel back the layers and acknowledge our truths. The goal is to balance, identify and create an understanding of the good, bad, and ugly within. Are you ready, my friend? Remember, you set the pace. The intention is to go beyond the surface, to get really uncomfortable. In my experience, you must revisit every good book in different seasons in your life. The book's impact varies depending on the different seasons or transitions we are in. Freedom from fear, the guide introduction to shadow work, is one of those books. Take what resonates and leave what does not. Trust the rest will be there when you need it. The shadow work process truly requires a lot from us on an emotional level. No suppressing, avoidance, coping with toxic people, toxic traits, or toxic behaviors. No romanticizing, no escapism, no more limiting beliefs controlling your destiny. Shadow work is intended to help us identify our dark side. Create understanding and accountability, and acceptance.

The beast inside is just seeking to be loved by you. The side that we do not want the world to see and that we may hold shame, guilt, etc. This is a side of us we keep buried deep within us, the beast. The dark side holds traits and behaviors that do not serve us and create blockages and prevent us from growing, glowing, expanding, and aligning with our highest self.

Shadow's in the Darkness

Anger

Arrogance

Egotistical Energy

Avoidance

Overthinking

Anxious Energy

Frustration

Impatience

Hopeless Energy

Exhaustion

Burnout

Fear

Behaviors of the Beast

- Defensiveness
- Envy
- Jealousy
- Fear based thinking
- Intolerance
- Judgmental
- Manipulative
- Controlling
- Obsessive tendencies
- Self-centered
- Self-sabotaging
- Stubborn

This work is crucial. Digging deep and staring the beast in the face is required. This process helps you to release and remove blockages that have been holding you back. It's time to address All your narratives and confirm if they are serving you or creating a hindrance in your present-day life. I trust that you will release, renew or restore all narratives. The beauty in this process is that once you identify the narratives created , you're able to renew, release, and restore all of your relationships and outlooks. Our dreams and goals, we have created for ourselves are refreshed and backed by love, not fear. The importance of this process is that when you let go of your limiting beliefs, you can operate at your highest vibration. This creates alignment for all that you desire.

At this point, you can recognize what are truly obstacles and what are truly opportunities and release fear. You deserve to show up in this world as your best self, free of fear and full of light and love! Please allow this book to be a tool to guide you on this shadow work path.

In the next chapter, I will provide numerous questions to help us through the stagnation and create life-changing momentum and awareness. The intention is to understand, accept and feel what's within. It's time to unleash the BEAST.

This is just a reminder this process will be difficult at times, always challenging; however, the rewards are priceless. I pray you will find confidence in your understanding. I pray you will find your authentic voice. I pray you decide to choose you my friend . I know you are worth doing the work! I trust you will find peace in the process. Just surrender and Trust; the time is Now.

I do suggest working with a licensed professional. Finding a wonderful therapist has impacted my entire world. I must say I breathe now with such ease. I mean that on a clinical level and, more importantly, on a spiritual level. The goal is love, peace, and harmony. A healthy balance between the mind, body, and soul.

TIME FOR PEACE AND PROTECTION:

Breath work: (3)

- Breathe In, count to three slowly, and fill your lungs!
- Now, hold your breath for three seconds
- Release, slowly exhale for three seconds
- Now, smile or laugh no matter your current emotions!

Crystal :(2)

Black Tourmaline

Enhances protection and purification & is an enteric vacuum cleaner by eliminating negativity.

Peridot

Sharpens the mind. Gives you the confidence to rely on yourself rather than on outside influences.

Affirmation:(1)

I make room for my personal growth.

CHAPTER 5

INTO
THE SHADOWS

Life has many more moments of darkness than we are all willing to discuss with one another. However, the lack of conversation doesn't stop the experiences nor the impact. We are learning this process to help fine harmony between the dark and the light moments. Balancing both is crucial to our existence. The Shadow Work process will get dark and emotionally difficult at times. I encourage you to focus on your feelings and what is true for you. I believe if you trust this process you will experience the most freedom at the end.

The goal is to deal and heal, my friend! This chapter of the book is sectioned into parts, with the intention's on being more digestible. I have cultivated these parts to make the shadow work easier and clear to process. Also, in hopes to encourage a beginner to take action and start.   Please remember that this chapter is self-paced, and please seek a professional whenever you feel overwhelmed.

DISCLAIMER:

I am not a license professional. This section isextremely triggering. Below are many writing prompts and questions. They have the power to bring suppressed memories back to the surface.I will encourage you to write letters to release some old emotions. You have a choice to burn, mail or keep these letters.When we deal, we heal; let's begin!

Parts of the DARKNESSES

Part 1 Shadow work

Part 2 Self-awareness

Part 3 Perception

Part 4 Core values

Part 5 Influence

Part 6 Trust

Part 7 Untruth

Part 8 Judgment

Part 9 Your Voice

Part 10 The Void

Part 11 Energy in motion = Emotions

Part 12 Past Trauma

Part 13 Avoidance

Part 14 Failure

Part 15 Fear

Part 16 Envy

Part 17 Self-Accountability

Part 18 Self-forgiveness

Help to move through your feelings

- Please seek a qualified healthcare provider

- No rush; trust the process

- Set the book down and walk away as needed!

- Get up and move your body for 10 minutes in the moment to transmute the energy immediately

Heart Rate Check

Do I feel triggered by this question?

Why?

Write about how you feel.

Write about the facts.

Do I Need more time to process my emotions and thoughts?

Set the book down, go for a 10-minute walk, or move your body for 10 minutes.

Is this something I would like to table until my next appointment with my therapist?

Write about what comes up and leave it in a journal you use during therapy, then discuss it in the next session.

Part 1 shadow work

What does the term 'Shadow Work' mean to you?

Do you understand that this work will take a lifetime?

Are you ready to Trust the Process of shadow work?

Describe how you would like to feel after starting your shadow work process.

Part 2 self-awareness

Write your definition of integrity.

Do you have integrity?

Describe your conscious knowledge of your character.

What are your preconceptions about femininity?

What are your preconceptions about masculinity?

Describe how these energies show up in your life daily.

Have you been doing the best with what you know and how you feel?

Describe the meaning of life.

Write about who you are.

How do you feel about who you are as a human?

Are you Proud of the human you are today?

Describe your mindset.

Write about if your mindset is thriving.

Why or why not?

Write about what limiting beliefs you have.

Describe how these limiting beliefs affect your life daily.

Describe the first signs that your mental health is declining?

Write about what happiness means to you.

Today, at this moment, do you consider yourself happy?

Why or why not?

Create a timeline of impactful events you have experienced in life from birth to now.

Describe what is holding you back from living a life of freedom and joy.

Part 3 Perception

What do you think are negative character traits?

What do you think are positive character traits?

Describe how you demonstrated these traits daily.

How would you want your loved ones and close friends to describe your character?

How do you think your loved ones and close friends describe your character?

Ask a few of your love ones and close friends to describe your character.

How do you think other people experience you?

What are the facts about your character?

Write about the facts of your perception of the people around you.

Describe your perception of yourself.

Write about why your perception is the way it is.

Part 4 Core values

Write your definition of core values.

Identify the importance of having core values.

Describe your core values.

How do your core values show up in your day-to-day life?

How do your core values show up in all your relationships.

Write about what you are morally passionate about.

Write about your highest priorities as a human being show-ing up in today's world.

Write about how your core values represent you.

Describe the beliefs you hold deep in your heart.

Describe what fundamentally drives you as a human being in today's world.

Write about your parent's/guardian's core values.

Do you hold these today, or do they differ?

Describe how they differ.

Part 5 Influence

Write about the authority figure that had the most negative influence on you growing up.

Write about the authority figure that had the most positive influence on you growing up.

Describe the person who had the most effect on your character.

Describe who impacted the development of your present-day behaviors.

As a child, were you ever asked how you felt emotionally by an authority?

Write a letter to your younger self about your childhood influence and their present-day effects on your life now.

Identify some major influences that you remember and hold possible trauma.

Write about the toxic traits you have recognized in your childhood authority figures and the impact.

Identify and write about your toxic behaviors and traits now.

Part 6 Trust

Identify and write your definition of trust.

Are you a trustworthy person?

Write in detail why or why not.

Write about your first experience with trust.

Describe who you felt as a child you could put all your trust in.

Write about how this relationship has impacted your adult perceptive as it relates to trust.

Write about the example of trusting behavior you had in your childhood.

Write bout one time you've felt betrayed as a child.

Write about how this has affected you in your adulthood.

What would you like to communicate to the person who broke your trust?

Describe how you feel when you trust someone.

Write about how being able to trust another person makes you feel.

Do you trust yourself?

Part 7   Untruth

Describe your definition of telling a lie.

Describe how you feel when you find out others have decided not to tell you the truth.

Write about how you felt when someone you trusted told you a lie.

Describe how this changed or impacted the relationship.

Write about what you constantly lie to yourself about.

What's the biggest lie you've ever told, and why?

Write about how this lie has impacted your life today.

Describe any fears you have about using speaking your authentic truth.

Part 8   Judgment

Describe your definition of a judgmental person.

Are you a judgmental person?

Are you afraid of being judged by others?

Write about your internal fear of judgment.

Describe how you respond when being judged by others.

Describe the areas and/or aspects of your life you are hiding from the people around you, including your loved ones, in fear of being judged.

Write about why you are afraid to show people these aspects of your life.

When do you find yourself being judgmental?

Describe how you feel when you are being judgmental.

Part 9 Your Voice

Describe how you were taught to use your voice as a child.

Write about how this has impacted your voice today.

Write about what fears you have around using your authentic voice.

Write about how you think your authentic voice sounds to yourself and others.

Are you assertive?

Are you direct?

Are you truthful?

Are you shy?

Are you timid?

Are you fearful?

Write about a time you suppressed your voice to make others comfortable.

Describe how you felt,did you feel good or bad?

Describe how you would handle that same situation moving forward.

Describe how you feel about +confrontation.

Identify how your feelings in regards to confrontation impact your voice.

What was the last argument you had about?

Was it resolved?

What is something that you've always wanted to confront someone about?

Why haven't you?

Do you plan to?

Why?

Write a letter to this person now, do not suppress your voice.

Describe how you plan to use your authentic voice moving forward.

Part 10 The Void

Describe a time you felt a void in your life.

Write about how you filled that void.

Write about what emptiness feels like to you.

Describe healthy strategies you might develop to overcome feelings of emptiness.

Identify the facts around the void's you fill.

Part 11 Energy in motion = Emotions

Write your definition of emotional maturity.

Are you emotionally mature?

Write about your earliest memories of your gardens expressing emotions.

Describe how you were taught to identify your emotions as a child.

How do you navigate your emotions now?

Identify the hardest emotion it is for you to feel and experience.

Write about why you feel this is?

Describe how you processed emotions as a child, teenager, and young adult.

Write about how this behavior has changed over time.

Talk about how you process negative emotions now.

What negative emotions do you tend to avoid?

Write about why you decide to avoid these emotions.

Describe a time you were asked how you felt after major life events and or changes, such as a major move, dealing with death and loss, etc.

Do you ever have physical reactions to emotional feelings?

Identify and write about these physical reactions.

Why do you think this happens? What is your body trying to tell you?

Are you listening to your body?

* Anger / Energy in motion

Please describe your definition of anger.

Do you feel angry often?

Write about if you identify when you feel anger in the moment or after the moment has passed.

Write about if you are comfortable with expressing anger or do you usually suppress your feelings of anger.

Write about what triggers your anger to arise.

Describe a time you were hurt and not angry.

Describe what you feel when feelings of annoyance arise.

Describe what you feel when feelings of displeasure arise.

Describe what hostility feels like in your body.

Are you pleased with your actions when you feel angry?

Why or why not?

Part 12- Past Trauma

Write your definition of trauma.

Have you felt deeply distressed in the past?

Have you had a deeply disturbing experience in the past?

Describe any past traumas; please write about how they have affected your life today.

How do you carry the pressure of your past trauma?

What person has hurt you the most in your life?

Write them a letter telling them everything you'd like to communicate to them.

Do you feel safe?

Peace project: look in a mirror and tell your inner child that you are not alone and that you are safe.

Part 13 Avoidance

Write about what you avoid thinking about, feeling, or doing.

Write about your avoidance tendencies.

Describe your daily avoidance behaviors.

Write about any family avoidance patterns you fear repeating.

Write about how you romanticize your life.

Do you ever find yourself manipulating people to avoid personal beliefs and or protect yourself?

When you think about it, is there any area of your life you're in denial about?

Do you often find yourself overthinking what you've said or how you've acted?

What usually triggers this behavior?

Part 14 Failure

Write about how you perceive failure.

Identify and write your definition of failure.

How do you feel when you feel you have failed?

Write about your fear of failure.

How did your parents/guardians respond to failure?

Write about what you consider to be your most impactful failure in your life.

What are the facts about this failure?

Describe the lessons you learned.

Are you prepared to decide to move forward?

Why or why not?

Write about if you can decide to surrender to this feeling of failure.

Part 15 Fear

Identity and write about your definition of fear

Identify and write about what makes you feel in danger.

Write about the facts of the last dangerous experience you experienced.

Describe a person or place you feel is dangerous.

Describe a situation that you feel can cause you pain.

Write about a time you felt threatened by a person, place, or situation.

Do you feel being in danger, harmed, or threatened often?

Write about why.

Write about if you feel safe alone.

Write about your level of safety as a child.

Describe the impact of these feelings in your adult life today.

Describe any fears you feel around change.

Describe any fears you feel around abandonment.

Describe any fears you feel around rejection.

Identify and write about your deepest fear.

What are the facts about this fear you have?

How might you be able to expose yourself to that fear in a safe way?

Are your ready to allow yourself to feel safe in 99.9% of situations that occur your life, and only express fear when you are in danger based off factual information and events ?

This healthy lifestyle is an option, if you create and choose it.

Part16 Envy

Identify and write your definition of envy?

How do you describe envious people?

Are you an envious person?

Write about if you generally feel less than, better than, or equal to others.

What makes you feel envy?

Write about a time you felt envious of another person.

Who do you envy and why ?

Describe your first example of envious behaviors you experienced in your childhood.

What tends to trigger you to feel envious?

Why do you think this is?

Do you desire to release feelings of envy?

Part 17 Self-Accountability

Identify and write your definition and feelings around self-accountability.

Describe how you hold yourself accountable daily.

Do you set realistic goals you know you'll be willing and capable of accomplising?

Write about how you hold yourself accountable for your actions.

Write about how you hold yourself accountable for your behaviors.

Describe how you take responsibility for your emotional experience.

Do you hold yourself accountable for enforcing your boundaries with other people?

Do your respect and honor other people's boundaries?

Please write about the most hurtful thing you've done to yourself.

Talk about the facts around this hurtful thing you did to yourself.

Are you ready to hold yourself accountable and forgive yourself?

Are you ready to move forward after hurting yourself?

What's the most hurtful thing you've ever done to someone else?

Have you ever apologized to this person?

Why or why not?

Write a letter apologizing to yourself or write a letter forgiving yourself, or both.

Part 18 Self-forgiveness

Identify and write your definition of forgiveness.

Do you practice self-forgiveness?

How often do you forgive yourself for your actions?

How often do you forgive yourself for your self-talk?

Write about what kind of things do you feel you need to be forgiven for? Why is this?

Write about a time when you needed forgiveness.

What are the facts about this experience?

Did you ask to be forgiven?

Did you apologize?

How did the situation play out at the end?

Are you okay with the outcome?

Describe if you were brought up to value self-forgiveness.

Do you forgive other people with ease?

Self-love project:

What is your definition of self-care?

Are you ready to love yourself fully, the good and the bad, the dark and the light?

ou are ready to surrender and trust your ance of your heart.

re prepared to allow and receive the abun- round you.

rfect self-care day.

What bringsyou joy daily?

What makes you feel happy?

Who are you?

What do you like?

What do you not like?

What are your established boundaries?

What self-care do you regularly practice daily, weekly, monthly?

- Journaling

- Conversation

- Working with a therapist

- Seek healing rituals and or drop to your knees in prayer and call in your ancestors

TIME FOR PEACE AND PROTECTION:

Breath work: (3)

- Breathe In, count to three slowly, and fill your lungs!
- Now, hold your breath for three seconds
- Release, slowly exhale for three seconds
- Now, smile or laugh no matter your current emotions!

Crystal :(2)

Azurite

Self-Expression, Enhanced Enlightened Thinking, helps to relieve stress.

Hiddenite

Protective, Improved self-awareness, communication Heralds expansion, and growth. Promotes harmonious and compassionate living.

Affirmations:(1)

I AM safe, and I AM enough

CHAPTER 6

DUALITY AND FREEDOM

The IMPORTANCE of shadow work is to create an understanding and acceptance   that we all have a light and darkness within. Honestly, it is a part of the human experience. Shadow work helps us to navigate this duality. I Have found creating this balance within myself extremely peaceful. I understand that everything bad that has happened for me or may happen for me in the now is for my good. I also know not to focus too much on the future because I can't concentrate on any true facts. Life is a process, and the only promise is continuous change. I approached every situation with ease and seek out the lesson. I have to ask myself why did I write this in my story. What about this person's place or experience, did I feel was necessary for the elevation of my soul?

A healthy, balanced mindset can help us look at problems as an opportunity to grow. It's time to answer all our internal questions with a healthy truthful answer. Standing in our authentic truth and gaining back the authority over our life is extremely empowering and necessary to live without fear. During this process, we release fear we choose to surrender. Our heart finds freedom and creates a safe place for our inner and outer child to co-exist. Our adult self becomes the authority. It's our mindset that has to be reconciled, renewed, restored, and rebuilt. This is a reminder that shadow work takes a lifetime.

Trust me; I had many layers to uncover, even some that were established in the first grade. I would love to give you an example of my required shadow work. When I was a young child, I had many undiagnosed learning disabilities. I'm thankful for my grandparents taking action and getting me tested and properly diagnosed before entering the fifth grade. The public school system just kept pushing me forward, although I was failing. When I did go to the fifth grade, I was at a second-grade reading level. I did not know how to read or write. My teachers would isolate me from the rest of the students in the class in a horrible attempt to make me, an ADHD student, more manageable for their ease. The school failed me. My teachers failed me. I was scared and hurt most days drowning in isolation, confusion, embracement, and shame. Being the only African American student with no explanations or understanding of my multitude of learning disabilities. I felt stupid. I felt shamed. I was forced to feel lonely in my learning environment. The authorities over me in the school environment failed me. I built a negative narrative and many limiting beliefs. I continue to live my life though lenses I created based off these experiences and what was happening to me and how I was being treated. These lenses made me crave being a perfectionist and a know it all. Always seeking to be the smartest person in the room. Never taking risk too afraid to fail and be judged by others. Never feeling alive. One limiting belief was that I was not worthy of others' time and attention. I became a child and then an adult sacred to take up space in my own life and the people around me. I mastered all the people-pleasing skills to survive. Shadow work has helped me identify and release the lies and the limiting beliefs. It also helped me to release the avoidance and escapism behaviors I used to cope with my day-to-day life. These patterns no longer served me. I have renewed and released my understanding of the situation. My teacher did not understand how I needed to be educated and failed me as a student. That is not my weight to carry; it is theirs! I had to restore my belief in myself and my worthiness. I recognize I no longer have to live trying to make these feelings from childhood my adult truth. I have rebuilt my mindset to know I deserve to be here and anywhere I am, just like the next human being that woke up with oxygen in their lungs. I released all negative feelings and fears of being inadequate to others. I now take imperfect yet impactful action daily. I walk in rooms fearless ready to listen and learn. After working with my therapist, I can now show up as the Queen of my palace, backed by many of my ancestors and in my own power and strength. Embodying self-confidence, self-efficacy, and self-love. I lead by example, showing everyone it is their birthright to take up space in this world now and forever.

Okay, friends, you must have a plan to identify and deal with your emotions. I have found it helpful to have systems in place like tabling conversations for later with my therapist, journaling, and walking outside to reset. You have to find your healthy outlets. Please seek professional help if you feel overwhelmed by this process. Honestly, having a therapist to speak with during this process has made it extremely digestible.

Take time to acknowledge the process is difficult. However, it is also worth it because you can find yourself aligned with your purpose and peace. I love my new life; I enjoy living each day! Now, I have new eyes! Everything I feel comes through the heart now and is feeling-based, and not thought-based thoughts are man-made. Feelings are delivered from God, Source, the Universe created, and rooted in love. Life is too short not to enjoy it to the fullest, do the work, friend live a life without fear and full of joy and abundance. The only person that can free you is you!

TIME FOR PEACE AND PROTECTION:

Breath work: (3)

- Breathe In, count to three slowly, and fill your lungs!

- Now, hold your breath for three seconds

- Release, slowly exhale for three seconds

- Now, smile or laugh no matter your current emotions!

Crystal :(2)

Black Sapphire

Deflecting negativity attracts prosperity and successful enterprises. Promotes Confidence and courage.

Moss Agate

Herald new beginnings and ideas. Encourages a sense of tranquility and emotional balance.

Affirmation:(1)

Changing my beliefs change my life

BLIND FAITH AND BOUNDARIES

Anew dialogue is required; you have to acknowledge fears and ensure you are not showing up as the Bad cop and the Good cop in your life. This type of duality makes it hard to embody self-trust and integrity. The goal is to set firm and necessary boundaries. This creates the perfect environment for an authentic lifestyle. A life with harmony, self-awareness, self-accountability, and self-acceptance.

I'm going to be honest; most of our internal self-talk is trash! We would never speak to people; we love how we speak to ourselves. This internal abuse has to end now! Listen, I had to look in a mirror one day. I had a team meeting. I said Me, myself and I front and center. In my best, I mean business voice. At this point, I was speaking out loud and staring intensely in my eyes in the mirror . Then I took time to allow my soul to speak to my inner child, aka little miss. Era and my out child aka trouble Tee. I said look, you all, we are all we have now and forever. I said no one is getting into the grave with us, so as our only true lifelong friends, we must be kinder to ourselves. Do We understand? Looking dead straight at myself in the mirror and waiting for a response. Yes, I'm completely aware I sound like a proper crazy lady. Don't judge just listen because it worked. I took 3 deep breaths and knew by the peace that came over my heart that the message was received loud and clear. My new friends listen. I'm now able to set concrete boundaries and speak from my authentic truth, but it's a newfound conference and peace. I have integrity and love. I'll be honest, friend this is daily difficult work. I make micro choices to do only actions and behaviors that serve me now. Actions that will serve my future self.

When we take responsibility for our thoughts, we take responsibility for our actions. In this cycle of accountability, we release the energy of fear and take responsibility for our time here on earth. When was the last time you felt alive my friend?

I was able to recognize I was on auto pilot thinking I was growing and changing. Let's be clear I was automatically moving in no direction and calling it success and love and happiness. Friend my heart were in prison and my head was consuming poison daily. It's time to heal our hearts and emotions so we can stand tall in our power. You are worthy of the life you know you deserve. You can decide to do the shadow work and live a life with less fear daily. Time to spread love within, don't be afraid to pull your energy back. Start asking yourself how you feel in every moment, then allow room for forgiveness and grace!

TIME FOR PEACE AND PROTECTION:

Breath work: (3)

- Breathe In, count to three slowly, and fill your lungs!
- Now, hold your breath for three seconds
- Release, slowly exhale for three seconds
- Now, smile or laugh no matter your current emotions!

Crystal :(2)

Jet

Clears the energy field of negative emotional attachments. Heal's aura energy leaks. Helps with protection, purification, and grounding.

Serpentine

Enables you to take control of your life rather than feel at the mercy of fate. Promotes self-empowerment.

Affirmation:(1)

I Am filled with confidence and good intentions.

CHAPTER 8

BE UNAPOLOGETIC, YOU ARE THE STAR OF THIS SHOW

Hey, my friends, this work is real. You have to take your time, move slow and be intentional. Please know that you might have to pick this book up and put it down twenty one times. Let me tell you something, friend, that's okay; allow yourself to be a beginner at this shadow work process. We are seeking an equally matched interval and external harmony. Peace is power! Say it with me. I desire and deserve to stand in daily peace and have a life full of harmony. Please decide to stand with me in this magical space.

The love we search for that deep understanding, that deep acceptance that unconditional love, is only found by going deep within. Take time to pause and process. Shadow work will help guide us on the path to release blockages that hold us back from experiencing life. It's time to allow ourselves to love. We are uniquely created to embrace freedom and take risk it's time. When we release fear, we can transmute it to empower ourselves daily. Show up in the world fearlessly! Take the stage and be the star! This is your experience; live and love, my friend, and most importantly, never stop learning and laughing! Let's Go!

TIME FOR PEACE AND PROTECTION:

Breath work: (3)

- Breathe In, count to three slowly, and fill your lungs!
- Now, hold your breath for three seconds
- Release, slowly exhale for three seconds
- Now, smile or laugh no matter your current emotions!

Crystal :(2)

Snowflake Obsidian

cleans and removes negative energy from our bodies and environment.

Lapis Lazuli

Encourages freedom from negative thoughts, thereby enhancing truthful communication, inner peace, and royal virtues.

Affirmation:(1)

I enjoy my positive thoughts and good feelings.

CHAPTER 9

CONGRATULATIONS, YOU ARE COMPLETE!

Whoop whoop, congratulations, you made it to the end. Please simultaneously allow this time to be the beginning of a new, healed, and higher vibrating version of yourself! I AM beyond proud of you! This work is extremely difficult however tremendously rewarding. Please set the best pace for you to revisit and continue doing the required maintenance. Don't forget to go back at your leisure as required. I have cultivated this chapter for your personal use. Below is the beginning of a notes section; please feel free to use it as your heart guilds you.

Ciao until we align again, with love T.C

PS.

If you need me, I'll be at The Unapologetic Palace Podcast!

* found on all podcast streaming platform's

TIME FOR PEACE AND PROTECTION:

Breath work: (3)

- Breathe In, count to three slowly, and fill your lungs!
- Now, hold your breath for three seconds
- Release, slowly exhale for three seconds
- Now, smile or laugh no matter your current emotions!

Crystal :(2)

Smokey Quartz

Enhance transmutation of negative energy and manifesting of dreams. Detoxify the body and energy field from lower vibrations. Disperses fear and lifts negativity and depression.

Chalcedony

Bestows on you an enthusiastic outlook on life

Affirmation:(1)

I trust the Divine timing of my life.

Dealing and Healing

Congratulations, You are Complete!

Congratulations, You are Complete!

Congratulations, You are Complete!

Congratulations, You are Complete!

Congratulations, You are Complete!

Congratulations, You are Complete!